THE GOSPEL IN COLOSSIANS

TIMOTHY DWYER

Topical Line Drives
Volume 44

ENERGION PUBLICATIONS
Gonzalez, Florida
2020

Unless otherwise marked, Scripture quotations taken from the New American Standard Bible® (NASB), Copyright © 1960, 1962, 1963, 1968, 1971, 1972, 1973, 1975, 1977, 1995 by The Lockman Foundation.
Used by permission. www.Lockman.org

Scriptures marked AT are the author's translation.

ISBN: 978-1-63199-734-1
eISBN: 978-1-63199-735-8

Energion Publications
PO Box 841
Gonzalez, FL 32560

https://energion.com
pubs@energion.com

INTRODUCTION

Colossians is about the supremacy, greatness, and all sufficiency of Christ. It is a direct challenge to those who would add to, or subtract from, the gospel of Christ in all its fullness. What is that fullness? Let us consider it in five stages: the background, God's plan, human sin, the work of Christ, and the new life in Christ's kingdom.

CHAPTER ONE

THE BACK STORY

The place to start to fully understand the greatness of Christ is the Torah, the first five books of the Bible. Genesis through Deuteronomy is the base story of the gospel in Colossians. Though Colossians contains no direct quotations from the Torah, the Torah is the prequel. The story is familiar, and from it, Colossians takes language to tell us about the work of Christ.

It starts with the **creation** of God. God deems creation "very good" (Genesis 1:31). Central in creation is the first man and women, created in the "**image** and likeness of God," according to Genesis 1:26-28. They are to rule over the earth: birds, fish, and land animals. God blesses them.

Sin invades the world, as it brings about a change in the condition of Adam and Eve. It is "crouching at the door" for Cain. It leads to a flood and the attempt to build a tower to the heavens. Adam and Noah both fail in their governing of the world.

God calls Abram. Abram is given a five-fold blessing (Genesis 12:1-3) and promised to become a mighty nation. At a crucial moment, Abram places **faith** in God, and that is credited to him as righteousness (Genesis 15:6). Through Isaac and Jacob and Joseph, the family grows into seventy people, and lands in Egypt, where they survive a famine, but become slaves.

God saves them by rescuing them from Egypt (Exodus. 14:30-31). They trust God and Moses. Then, God makes them a monumental offer: they can become a **kingdom** of priests and a **holy** nation (Exodus 19:4-6). They are God's **elect.** They are the chosen of the Lord, as Deuteronomy 7:6 says: "You are a holy people to the LORD your God; the LORD your God has chosen you to be a people for his own possession…" . As they leave Egypt, they are headed to a special **inheritance** in the land of Canaan that God has promised to give them. Exodus 32:13 speaks of the land they will inherit forever, as does Deuteronomy 1:38 and 3:28.

The key words from the Torah are vital for Colossians: **Creation, Image, Faith, Kingdom, Holy, Elect, Inheritance.** These words provide the grammar for the gospel story of Colossians. Paul, Peter, Timothy, and the other early Christians are so Story and Scripture saturated, that there is no way to tell the Jesus story apart from the Torah story.

Meanwhile, Israel disobeys. They wander in the wilderness for forty years, and then finally enter the land. They want a king, and God grants them one. The covenant offer for Israel to be a kingdom of priests and a holy nation is forgotten again and again, and the covenant stipulations in the law are forgotten again and again. As Lev. 26 and Deuteronomy 28 warned, exile is the result. They return, and try to survive the various rulers: Persians, Macedonian-Greeks, and Romans. Then, *He* comes. The One through whom all things were **created,** who is the **image** of the invisible God, who calls people to **faith,** invites them into his **kingdom.** He is forming a **holy, elect** people, who have an **inheritance** with all the saints in glory.

With the arrival of Jesus there is the message of a gospel, good news. It is rooted in the language of Isaiah (Isaiah 40:9, 41:27, 52:7, 61:1). It is announced by Jesus when he says that "The Spirit of the Lord is upon me, because he has anointed me to bring good news to the poor" (Luke 4:18-19, quoting Isaiah 61:1/ 58:6). Jesus' message is summarized as the gospel (cf. Mark 1:14-15).

With the death and resurrection of Jesus, the gospel message is set loose in the world to do its work. The apostles and others preach and teach it in Acts. Saul of Tarsus (aka Paul) is called, like Jeremiah or Moses of old, and travels from place to place planting communities of faith. He is Scripture-saturated, hard-working, trouble-prone, and the impression one gets is that with Saul, there is no better friend, and no worse enemy.

He is moving constantly west, from Asia minor to Macedonia and Greece, eventually to Rome, and probably as far as Spain. He is a great networker, with disciples and friends like Luke, Timothy, Phoebe, Junia and others. Some fail him and abandon him, while others carry on the same work, spreading the gospel and planting communities of faith.

Such is a man named Epaphras, who works in Asia minor in the territory around Laodicea and Hierapolis. He is only mentioned a few times in the Bible, in Colossians 1:7, 4:12, and Philemon 23. His name is a shortened form of Epaphroditus.

In Colossians 1:7, Epaphras is called "a beloved fellow slave" by Paul. Rather than the milder term "servant," Epaphras is one who was owned by Jesus Christ, who could say, " I have been crucified with Christ, it is no longer I who live, but Christ who lives in me," just as Paul could (Galatians 2:20). He did not belong to himself any more, for he had been bought with a price (1 Corinthians 6:19-20).

Paul goes on to say that Epaphras was faithful for the Colossians, a slight shift from the more usual sense of being faithful to God. He is also called a *diakonos tou Christou,* a server of the Messiah. One remembers that in Mark 10:43 that the one who would be great was to be a *diakonos.* In Matthew 23:11, Jesus said that the greatest was the *diakonos.*

In Colossians 4:12, Epaphras is once more called a *doulos Christou,* a slave of the Messiah. There is it noted that he always agonizes (*agōnizomenos*) for the Colossians in his prayers. He is "one of them." He has great pain (*polun ponon*), but that is part of a wider mission to Laodicea and Hierapolis, as well as Colossae.

The third and last time Epaphras is mentioned in the NT is in Philemon 23, also written to Colossae and the house church there which included Philemon, Archippus, Aphia, and others. Paul sends them greetings from Epaphras, whom he calls his "fellow-soldier." At this point, Epaphras had moved on from Colossae, and was with Paul, perhaps in Ephesus or Rome.

We can posit this movement. Around the mid-50s of the first century CE, Paul spent about three years in Ephesus (Acts 19). During this time, the message spread, for Acts 19:10 says that "all who lived in Asia heard the word of the Lord, Jews and Greeks." Many believe that it was at this time that Epaphras took the message to Colossae, about 125 miles away from Ephesus, as well as to the neighboring towns of Laodicea and Hierapolis.

These towns have a delightful setting in the Lycus valley. To this day, it is a great tourist region, with many enjoying the natural hot springs in the area. What sort of town was Colossae?

Author Michael Trainor[1] gives us some details in a recent article. It sits near the Lycus River at the base of a mountain, Mt. Cadmus, which is the highest mountain in western Turkey, 11 miles from Laodicea, and 15 miles from Hierapolis. It was settled from the Chalcolithic period (c. 3500 BCE) all the way to the Byzantine period in 1100 CE. Though there is debate, the Hittites seem to have first mentioned it, and the historian Herodotus called it "a great city in Phrygia" (*Histories 7. 30. 1*), Trainor tells us. Xenophon called it "a populous city, both wealthy and large" (*Anabasis 1.2. 6*).

The city was on a strategic trade route and was famous for dyed wool of a special type, called *colossinus,* which perhaps gave the city its name. From the Roman period, in the first century CE, there is a funeral stele which depicts a family sitting around a table, holding bread, with a dog beneath. The inscription tells us this is the clan of Tatianos.

Trainor says that archaeologists, unfortunately, have shown little interest in Colossae. We do know that an earthquake destroyed much of the region in 60 or 62 CE. The earthquake is not mentioned in Colossians, perhaps because the area was rebuilt, or the letter was written slightly earlier.

We can envision Epaphras, perhaps with some co-workers, making the six or seven-day trip from Ephesus to evangelize in Colossae, Hierapolis, and Laodicea. In these towns, the gospel bears fruit, and at least two house churches are started, one in the house of Philemon in Colossae (cf. Philippians 1-2) and another in the house of Nympha, likely in Laodicea (Colossians 4:15). There was movement back and forth for about five or so years, and the Colossian Jesus-followers got to know Aristarchus, John Mark, Luke,

---

1   Michael Trainor, "Colossae: Colossal in Name Only?" BAR March/April, 2019, pp. 44-50.

Demas, and a man named Jesus or Justus (Colossians 4:10-14). These small, young churches were making their way with a few upsets from time to time, such as the theft or slipping away by Onesimus, a slave of Philemon. Around the same time that Paul writes the letter of Colossians, he writes to Philemon about reconciliation with Onesimus. Ephesians was also likely carried to the area as well.

Young (and old) churches have multiple problems, though. The next major one seems to be the aberrant teaching of a group in Colossae, that much of the book of Colossians seeks to correct. This teaching de-centered Jesus from his primacy in the lives of the Colossians. What was this teaching, and who taught it?

From Colossians 2:8-10 and 16-19 we have some indication:

> "See to it that no one takes you captive through philosophy and empty deceitfulness and through human traditions, according to the elements of the world and not according to Christ. In him all the fullness of the godhead dwells bodily and you are complete in him who is the head of all rule and authority" (AT).

> "Do not let anyone judge you in food or drink or feast day or new moon or Sabbath, which are a shadow of the things coming, the body of Christ. Do not let anyone trick you with supposed humility and worship of angels which they claim to have seen, puffed up in the mind of their flesh and not holding to the head, from whom the whole body (of Christ) grows with the growth which is from God, in every joint and ligament" (AT).

Questions abound from these passages. For example, should the expression be translated "worship of angels" or "worship with angels"? Either is possible in the Greek genitive construction. What is clear is that some in Colossae were adding things into the gospel teaching which the Colossians had learned from Epaphras, Luke, and others.

There are a myriad of proposals as to who these Colossian misleaders were. For convenience sake, let me group the proposals into four categories:

5

- Some sort of early gnostics or local mystery religions. It may have been connected with Judaism.
- Local Anatolian religion with an ascetic tendency.
- A form of Judaism. The mention of Sabbath and new moons point in this direction.
- Some type of mystical asceticism, limiting foods that could be eaten.

Also uncertain is whether these misleaders were from within the house churches or traveled from the outside. Did ideas "in the marketplace" seep into the local teaching? How accurately the ideas were reported to Paul is another question.

Paul then writes Colossians to help the young church get back on track with a Christ-centered, Christ-sufficient, Christ-exalting faith. To be more specific, Paul writes with Timothy, according to Colossians 1:1. However, the careful reader will note that in the first couple of paragraphs of the letter, the plural pronoun "we" dominates (cf. vv. 3, 4, 9). However, in Colossians 1:24 it turns to "I." We need not doubt that Paul is the major voice in this letter. It is sent to Colossae, which is at the crossing of several roads, with Tychicus (Colossians 4:7-8), who is probably carrying the letter to the Ephesians and the one to Philemon at the same time (Ephesians 6:21). As Paul arranges his thoughts in Colossians, he likely returns to things he had preached and taught, and returns to Israel's story, where we began.

Renowned scholar N.T. Wright, who has written a wonderful small commentary on Colossians, gives a fine description of the Colossian believers in his recent biography of Paul.[2] They know of the ancient Jewish hope that God would come and fill the world with divine glory. They are ten or twenty "oddly assorted people" who crowd into Philemon's house to pray, to invoke Jesus as they worship the one God, to break bread together, and intercede for one another and the world. The Messiah is actually there in their midst, "the hope of glory" (Colossians 1:27). This small group is like the temple itself, a dwelling for God and foretaste of what will one day fill and complete the whole universe.

---

2 N.T. Wright, *Paul: A Biography* (San Francisco: Harper One, 2018), p. 291.

As a basic outline of what Paul writes to this young and small church, Colossians consists of the following:

- A greeting and prayer in 1:1-14
- A poem on the greatness of Christ in 1:15-20
- A review of their transformation in 1:21-24
- Paul's goals in 1:25-28
- Be rooted in Christ without wavering in 2:1-23
- Life in the community of faith and at home in 3:1-4:6
- Greetings and news in 4:7-18.

In 95 verses, we have a letter to a young church pointing them to the greatness and sufficiency of Christ and the gospel. At the heart, however, is that story of Israel we have mentioned.

Creation is in Christ, and all things are created for Christ and through Christ (Colossians 1:16). Early myths of creation can be forgotten, as can the idea of creation being manipulated by beings other than its creator.

The Image of God, originally in the first humans (Genesis 1:26-28) is embodied, or made human, in Christ (Colossians 1:15). He is the image of the invisible God. Christ, in some sense, replaces Adam, or fulfills what Adam could and did not accomplish.

The Kingdom that Israel was invited to be (Exodus 19:4-6) and failed at, has come to fruition in Christ. When someone believes in the gospel, that person is transferred from the authority of darkness to the **kingdom of God's beloved son** (Colossians 1:13).

An elect and holy people was the goal of the covenant God made with Israel (Exodus 19:4-6), and this also has now come to its fullness in the creation of the people of Christ (Colossians 3:12) who are **elect and holy.**

Faith was the original response of Abraham to the call of God, and likewise, the people of God are known by their **faith, having believed** the gospel (Colossians 1:4, 23, 2:7).

An inheritance awaits. Just as Israel once journeyed to inherit the land of promise (Deuteronomy 1:38, 3:28), so now believers have the **inheritance** of the saints in light, shifting from the physical promise of land to one now located "in Christ" (Colossians 1:12).

The book of Colossians is retelling Israel's story, with its fullness in Christ. At the same time, it is telling a counter-story to that of the Roman empire, as Brian Walsh and Sylvia Keesmaat have emphasized.[3] Like almost everything in New Testament studies, of course this is debated. However in a world where accolades to Caesar were common, such as Myra in Asia minor, where an inscription read "The people of Myra [honor] the emperor Tiberius, the exalted god, son of exalted gods, lord of land and sea, the benefactor and savior of the entire world,"[4] it is hard not to see at least some indirect counter narrative in Colossians. This young and confused house church is part of something bigger and more wonderful than they have imagined. They are part of God preparing the universe, through the spread of the gospel, for the One for whom it was originally created. The mystery hidden for ages is now known, and it is Christ among them, the hope and certainty of glory (Colossians 1:26-27).

As we wind up this chapter, let us reconsider the authorship of Colossians. Sharp eyes will have noted my use of the name "Paul." Luke Timothy Johnson has recently made the point, in his important book *Constructing Paul: The Canonical Paul, vol. 1* (Grand Rapids: Eerdmans, 2020) that the authority of New Testament does not rest on authorship, but canonization. From that perspective, says Johnson, letters like Colossians are "letters of Paul" whatever the particular authorship mechanics (which may have been more complicated or communal than modern minds commonly realize).

3 Brian J. Walsh and Sylvia C. Keesmaat, *Colossians Remixed: Subverting the Empire* (Downers Grove: InterVarsity Press, 2004). For a challenge to Walsh and Keesmaat, cf. Allan Bevere, "Colossians and the Rhetoric of Empire: A New Battle Zone," in Joseph Modica and Scot McKnight, eds., *Jesus is Lord Caesar is Not: Evaluating Empire in New Testament Studies* (Downers Grove: InterVarsity Press, 2014), pp. 183-196.
4 Drew Strait, "Proclaiming Another King Named Jesus? The Acts of the Apostles and the Roman Imperial Cult(s)" in Modica and McKnight, p. 131.

CHAPTER TWO

GOD'S PLAN: SINGING THE FAITH

We are examining the nature of the gospel in Colossians in this book. The first mention of the gospel comes in Colossians 1:5, where it is called the word of truth (just as in Ephesians 1:13). The next verse, Colossians 1:6, is fascinating.

There is it mentioned by Paul that the gospel is "bearing fruit and multiplying." Another way to put it would be "bearing fruit and growing." The language is that of a tree, but there is also a clear echo of Genesis 1:22, where God tells the first humans to "be fruitful and multiply" (NASB) and fill the earth. In Colossians 1, by way of comparison, the gospel is taking on the blessing of God and carrying a power to fill the earth! The gospel is "the power of God to salvation" in Romans 1:16, and here in Colossians it carries new creational power.

A second reference is in Colossians 1:23, where Paul urges believers not to move away from "the hope of the gospel." That hope is explained a few verses later, in verse 27, where it is Christ among the believers, their hope of glory. So, the gospel provides the hope for the glory that awaits believers. What an encouragement that would be to those who may have recently suffered the devastation of the earthquake in Colossae (if written slightly after the earthquake) and those battling the idolatries of the Roman empire in Asia minor.

It should not necessarily be a surprise that these the only two explicit uses of the word "gospel" or *euaggelion* in Colossians. After all, content may or may not contain specific vocabulary. Careful reading indicates that the expression "word," which is probably shorthand for "word of truth" also refers to the gospel. In Colossians 1:25, Paul wants to fulfill the word. In Colossians 3:16, the word of Christ or message about Christ was to dwell in them richly. Paul requests prayer for the word to find an open door in Colossians 4:3. What does Paul mean by the word or the gospel?

We could go to 1 Corinthians 15:1-9, where there is the *kerygma,* or summary message of Christ having died (according to the Scriptures), being buried, and then being raised (according to the

Scriptures). This is one of many short summaries (such as the sermons in the book of Acts) of the longer verbal presentations that Paul and Epaphras made as they traveled and worked.

In Colossians itself, for a summary of the gospel, and God's plan, perhaps the best starting point is in the great poem of Colossians 1:15-20. As with the other poems or hymns in the letters of Paul (such as Philippians 2:5-11), there is a multitude of interpreters who have weighed in on the contents, and almost every issue of interpretation is questioned and debated. My proposal is that Colossians 1:15-20 is the summary of God's plan in Christ for the world.

Almost every commentary weighs the views on the authorship of the poem, and whether it is by Paul, or added. We will shortly see two views, one of which sees Paul as originally writing the poem, and the other less certain.

Here is the text, with its structure set out:

- "Who is the image of the invisible God
- **Firstborn** of all creation
- For in him all things were created
- **In the heavens and on the earth**
- The visible and the invisible
- Whether thrones or lordships
- Whether rulers or authorities
- All things through him and for him were created
- He himself is before all
- All things hold together in him
- He is the head of the body, the church
- Who is the ruler
- **Firstborn** from the dead
- In order that in all things he might be first
- Because in him all the fullness was pleased to dwell
- And through him to reconcile all things to him
- Making peace through the blood of his cross
- **Whether on the earth or in the heavens**.

The poem seems clearly to be divided up into two sections, marked off by the terms "firstborn" and the reference to earth and heaven in each section. The first part focuses on the preeminence of Christ in creation, for all things were for Christ and through Christ, including the "rulers and authorities." These will come into play again in Colossians 2:10, where Christ is said to be head of them. In Colossians 2:15, the rulers and authorities are stripped of power. Clearly, 1:15-20 is setting the stage for things to be said later in the letter.

This preeminence in creation is related in the first half to preeminence in the church, the *ekklēsia,* or assembly of God's people. Paul will return to the church in Colossians 1:24, where it is again said to be Christ's body. All the body grows with a growth from God, in Colossians 2:19. The church in Nympha's house is mentioned in Colossians 4:15. This letter, and one to the Laodiceans, are to be swapped, according to 4:16, and each read, an indication of the connected network of churches.

The second half of the poem focuses on the reconciliation which the work of Christ created. It again focuses on the cosmic scale ("in heaven and on earth").

Christ is again called the "firstborn," a term used for preeminence in the Bible (cf. Psalm 89:27, Revelation 1:5, rather than for a literal birth or generation). Christ is "firstborn" from the dead, to have preeminence in all things, and effect reconciliation through the blood of the cross, to everything in heaven and on earth.

Perhaps two of the best explanations of the poem of Colossians 1:15-20 have been given in recent years by N.T. Wright, and Elliott Maloney. First, let us consider what Wright proposes.[5]

The poem has typically Pauline emphasis such as "Christological monotheism" just like Philippians 2:5-11, but also integrates Jewish wisdom traditions. Wright notes the obvious parallel expressions, mentioned abo, and sees an ABBA structure, a chiasm, with the following

---

5 N.T. Wright, "Poetry and Theology in Colossians 1:15-20," NTS 36(1990)444-468, repr. in *The Climax of the Covenant: Christ and the Law in Pauline Theology* (Minneapolis: Fortress, 1991).

- A vv. 15-16
- B v. 17
- B v. 18ab
- A vv. 18c-20
- The hinge is the
use of two key
expressions:
"in the heavens and earth"//
"He himself"//
"He himself"//
"in the earth and in the heavens." The parallel terms set
the poem in four sections.
- The backdrop is the Hebrew scriptures, where the term
"beginning" (*reshith*) is found in both Genesis 1:1
and Proverbs 8:22. Paul is taking traditional wisdom
thought, and combining with the developing Jewish idea
that there is both an insistence on the one true God,
and that this God is not a national deity, but Lord of all
creation. The one God has both the right and obligation,
because of the covenant, to step in and rescue his people
from their oppressors.
- Two things are held together theologically. One is the
complete humanness of Jesus, and the other is the complete identification with God. God's purpose is to sum
up all things in the man Jesus, but Jesus is also both
identified with and as God and separate from God.

The poem sets itself against traditional synagogue Judaism,
which may have been enticing the Colossians, and pagan religion
with its polytheism and dualism. Wright says the poem has the
same essential thought that undergirds all of Paul's letters: monotheism and election, redefined by means of Christology.

What can we say of Wright's proposals?

They are theologically rich, and exegetically full. There is the
need, however, to integrate the poem more specifically into Colossians. Let me propose two ways. First, in Colossians 1:10, Paul
has prayed for them to increase in the knowledge of God. One
concrete way this is possible is to see God in divine fulness, which

includes Christ. A second way is in terms of Paul's ministry goal of Colossians 1:28, where he instructs with all wisdom (including the wisdom background of this poem) so that each one would be complete in Christ. The only ways to be complete in Christ, and not looking beyond to Sabbath, new moons, or food laws, is to know the complete Christ, as set out in this poem. To say it a slightly different way, the fullness of this complete Christ overshadows fully any humanly devised attempts at "philosophy or empty deceit" involving rules like "do not taste, do not touch" (Colossians 2:8, 21).

There is another related issue from the whole of Colossians. If the powers, or "rulers and authorities and principalities" so familiar from Ephesians 6:10-12, were predominant in the lives and thinking of believers in Asia minor, it would make sense that both Colossians and Ephesians would address their proper place. Christ's supremacy as presented in the poem includes rulership over these beings. The way is not paved for the teaching about their defeat, and ultimate irrelevance (Colossians 2:14-15). Colossian believers need not fear them, take steps to thwart them or try and manipulate them. Nor should they be impressed with those who claim to control them. The spiritual powers are both created and defeated in Christ, part of Christ's supreme world conquering role destined and appointed from creation. The supremacy of Christ is both unchallenged and unrivaled, in ethics or theology.

A second proposal on the hymn by Elliott Maloney focuses on the desire of Paul to reorient the ways the Colossians thought and lived. He presents the wonderful idea that what is going on in Colossians 1:15-20 is that the author is correcting error with a song![6]

Christians have always sung their faith. Often, denominations have their own hymnals. There are a variety of hymns or songs in the NT, such as Philippians 2:5-11 and I Timothy 3:16, and many in the book of Revelation. The church father Ambrose is often credited with reviving or developing singing in the western church.

An odd twist is that a whole "worship industry" has sprung up in the last fifty years or so in the United States, often called Contemporary Christian Music, or CCM. Churches have often

---

6   Elliott C. Maloney, "Christ the Image of God and Head of the Church: The Christological Hymn of Colossians 1:15-20," *The Bible Today 51 (May, 2013)153-158.*

"gone contemporary" and turned down the lights with rock bands and concert-like settings.

My observation is that in many circles, the theology has devolved into "romance music" with "boyfriend Jesus" style songs. What has left the building is not Elvis, but Christology! The Colossian's hymn returns us to rich theology, as Maloney points out.

As has been mentioned, the false teaching combined some sort of asceticism (rules and religious rituals) with teachings on the "powers." Perhaps this meant ways of controlling the spiritual beings that inhabited the universe. Speculative philosophy had replaced theology in the quest for spiritual experience.

Like Wright, Maloney identifies two stanzas in the hymn (though he is less sure that the author is Paul). Stanza one focuses on the way that all things are united in Christ. Christ is preeminent, the manifest wisdom of God. The various ranks of angels or powers ("thrones and dominions") are familiar from Jewish writings such as *First Enoch,* and *The Testament of Levi.* God's plan for the salvation of all was from the dawn of creation, with Christ as supreme.

The second stanza points to the resurrection as the proof of God's love, says Maloney. This is the first stage of the full acceptance, or reconciliation. It is not nebulous celestial powers, but "the blood of the cross" that made peace.

The take-away is that Christ is the origin and center of our faith, and odd speculations or quests to know the other spiritual powers, or ascetic or religious practices which may be proposed to lead to a greater or deeper spirituality are greatly flawed. They take away and distract from the supremacy of Christ.

The implication is that the Colossians do not know enough about or have not gone deep enough into Christ. The religious buffet that Roman antiquity provided was only empty, fat calories. The hundred-plus options that someone in Colossae faced could not replace the greatness of Christ. The poem or song, and the rest of Colossians directs believers to their true foundation in the complete Christ.

The result? They can be walking trees, as the wonderful mixed metaphor of Colossians 2:6 points out. They are to walk in Christ, rooted and grounded as a tree would be, and built up as a building would be. It is in Christ that are hidden all the treasures of wisdom and knowledge (Colossians 2:3), not in the speculations of the religious smorgasbord around the Colossian believers.

The religious options only have multiplied with the advent of technology in our day. One can take in the religious teachings of a savant from across the world from the comfort of one's kitchen or living room. Are we still rooted and grounded in Christ?

As has been mentioned, this song is integrated into almost everything else that Paul says in Colossians. Let us take three more examples to see this.

Colossians 1:16 says that all things were **created** *(Gk.ektisthē)* in Christ, through Christ, and for Christ. Paul returns to that creation language in Colossians 3:10, where he says that believers are to put on the new person, who is being renewed according to the image of the One who **created** *(ktisantos)* that person.

In Colossians 1:18, in the song, it is noted that Christ is **the head of his body, the church** *(hē kephalē tou sōmatos tēs ekklēsias)*. Then, in Colossians 2:19, instead of turning to self-referential visions and angel worship one is to hold fast to **the head** *(tēn kephalēn)*, from which **the entire body** *(pan to sōma)* is held together and experience a growth that comes from God.

Then, there is Colossians 3:16 where the "word of Christ" is to dwell richly in believers. It is not clear grammatically if this is meant to be a word *about* Christ, or *Christ's words,* the objective or subjective genitive in the Greek. Less likely is a genitive of apposition, the word which is Christ (irregular outside of John). In light of Colossians 1:15-20 and the song we are considering, a good option is to think that the word of Christ refers to the song which is so central in the Colossian letter, and whose content reverberates throughout its whole message.

Our point is that the plan of God is summed up in the song, and the song takes preeminence of place in the letter. The prayers, ethics, community life, and theology are all rooted in the song.

The rest of the letter also keeps us from misunderstanding the song. For example, the song speaks of God reconciling all things, in Colossians 1:20. This language of reconciliation is picked up again in Colossians 1:22, where the believers are reconciled. However,

Colossians 3:5-6 also speaks of the wrath of God coming upon those who continue to practice idolatry, are covetous, and are fornicators. That is why believers must put to death those sins in their lives and not continue in them.

At this point, it may be helpful to review another element of the Colossian gospel. What was the religious or spiritual condition from which believers were rescued in Christ? What was their status and what was their life like apart from Christ? We will see that the picture was very bleak indeed.

CHAPTER THREE

LIFE APART FROM CHRIST

In the Old Testament, there are calls from the prophets to both the people of Israel and those outside to turn to God because of the divine wrath and sin. For example, Jonah famously says that Nineveh will be destroyed in forty days, but they turn to God, and the penalty is suspended. Hosea speaks of the violation of the ten commandments (Hosea 4:2). In the famous Psalm 51, there is a prayer to be cleansed from sin in v. 2.

In the ministry of Jesus, that pattern is followed. He spoke of people perishing unless they repented, for example, in Luke 13:1-9. People loved the darkness rather than the light, because their deeds were evil (John 3:19). His opponents were of their father, the devil, a murderer and a liar (John 8:44).

Letters that Paul wrote before Colossians, such as Romans, carried this same thought. Romans speaks of people being handed over to sin (Romans 1: 24, 26, 28). All are under sin (Romans 3:9). Sin is a slave master, a ruling power (Romans 5:21). How does Colossians follow this description of humans without the gospel?

We want to remember that Colossians is an "occasional" document, seeking to present the supremacy of Christ against deviations into focus on religious practices or philosophical speculations. It is not a treatise of systematic theology, nor are any of Paul's letters. Yet, it is rich in theology at the same time, practical theology oriented to helping people rejoice in Christ and experience love, unity, and holiness in the believing community. At times, the life the Colossians had been rescued from is mentioned. Here are some highlights, or lowlights, which probably came from Paul's or Epaphras's preaching.

- They were in the domain of darkness (Colossians 1:13)
- They were in need of redemption (just as the Israelites from Egypt, Colossians 1:14, Exodus 6:6)
- They needed the forgiveness of sins (Colossians 1:14)
- They were alienated and hostile of mind, practicing evil deeds (Colossians 1:21)

- They lacked reconciliation (Colossians 1:22)
- They were marked by transgressions against God (Colossians 2:13)
- They were dead in those transgressions, and in the uncircumcision of their flesh (2:13)
- They had decrees against them in a sort of certificate of debt held to their discredit (Colossians 2:14)
- They were under the elementary principles of the world (Colossians 2:20); a probably reference to earth, air, fire, and water and the belief that they controlled human destiny and needed to be placated constantly
- They were under the wrath of God for their sins (Colossians 3:6)
- They were characterized by an old person or self or nature, which was known for evil practices (Colossians 3:9)
- Lying seems to have been a constant part of their lives (Colossians 3:9)
- Ethnic distinctions were their identity markers (Colossians 3:11)
- Less explicit, but most likely assumed is the idea that they were controlled by "rulers and authorities" or spiritual powers (Colossians 1:16, 2:10, 2:15)

This is a very bleak picture indeed. At the same time, it is more dire than some gospel presentations make the human condition. People need more than good relationships and finances, or a moment of inner peace. At the same time, there are elements of the Roman world that would have certainly been present in the Colossian's lives that are not mentioned, such as the continued and unending quest for honor, use of magic and attempts to manipulate the spirit world, the idolatries of worship of the family gods or *lares,* and the ever present emperor worship in Asia minor.

Did they attend gladiator games with the blood lust and violence prevalent there? Were they participants in festivals to Bacchus with the drunkenness? Did those who were masters abuse or sexually mistreat their slaves? Was adultery viewed as unbinding on the *paterfamilias* if he consorted with prostitutes or slaves?

Another area of the lives of the Colossians can come into focus without Christ. It was mentioned above that there was an emphasis on reconciliation, both in the poem, where it says in Colossians 1:20 that through Christ there is the *reconciliation* of all things to him, and then two verses later, where it speaks of the Colossian believers now being *reconciled* in the body of Christ's flesh, through his death, to present believers holy and blameless before him.

Let us ponder briefly the issue of reconciliation and then the role of Colossian believers in relation to the Roman Empire under this topic of life apart from Christ.

A number of years ago, scholar Max Turner wrote a helpful article on reconciliation that has a proper range of consideration.[7] He combines Ephesians, Colossians, and Philemon in his focus. Why? Philemon is the famous case of the departure of Onesimus from the household of Philemon, with its setting in Colossae. Ephesians was written about the same time as Colossians, perhaps carried together with it, and indeed, there are many that believe that Ephesians borrowed from Colossians. Here are Turner's two key observations.

Turner says that the whole point of the gospel is to reverse the multiple alienations of the Fall. This means that reconciliation is not just about fixing bad social relationships, based on some dispute, but it indeed includes them (as with Onesimus). Fundamentally, the second observation is the larger one. It is that theologically reconciliation is also about reintegrating people who mirror or image the divine trinitarian personhood of loving unity and so demonstrate the grace of forgiveness exemplified in the Christ event.

What is the contribution of Colossians? Colossians sets Philemon on a broader canvas. Turner, following Dunn, notes that in the poem of 1:15-20, there is the unmentioned but assumed falling of the cosmos under the heavenly powers, mentioned in 1:13. This ongoing crisis is resolved in the cross. So, the defeat of these powers is the means of reconciling heaven and earth.

Colossians 1:22 has an intensive neologism for "reconcile," *apokatallassō*, found elsewhere only in the related Ephesians 2:16. It

---

7 Max Turner, "Human Reconciliation in the New Testament with Special Reference to Philemon, Colossians, and Ephesians," EurJTheol (2006)37-47.

is quite possibly Paul's own creation. The assumption is what Turner calls the "big plot," namely that there is a fractured and alienated creation. However, in the work of Christ, the eschatological harmony is already being inaugurated and *even made visible* in the church. From that perspective, the unity of Colossians 3:11, where ethic divides are bridged. This is the reason that the syncretistic, false teaching of mystical asceticism is so deadly. Not only does it set aside the completeness of life in Christ, but it reinstalls the old divisions. The new creation ethic of love, forgiveness, unity and peace, is lost in the shuffle.

Life apart from Christ is then fractured, alienated, and part of the great cosmic divide under the sway of the powers, principalities and rulers in the spirit world. It is the spirit world division of alienation which must be addressed by the work of Christ, reintegrating humanity into the new creation via reconciliation and unity in the body of Christ.

How were the Colossian's lives, embedded in the Roman empire, affected in this large-scale reconciliation? Let us return briefly to our earlier allusions to life in the Roman world.

There was a flurry of studies on the relation of the New Testament to the Roman empire in the 1990s, and the flurry has continued unabated. The first wave saw various NT writes countering the mythology and narrative of Roman greatness with "hidden transcripts," which flew below the radar, but were very subversive to traditional Roman order. Colossians has been examined from this perspective by two notable contributions.

We mentioned earlier Brian Walsh and Sylvia Keesmaat's book *Colossians Remixed,* which one reviewer called "a Molotov cocktail" of a book. More modestly, Harry O. Maier assessed Colossians and the Roman empire.[8] Both serve to remind us (whatever their limits) that life apart from Christ, as presented in Colossians (and the rest of the NT) is not only or merely about bad individual sins, such as swearing, but also about being embedded in systems which pull a person in particular directions, sometimes without awareness. The systems may offer power, rewards, and glory, but at the end of the

---

8   Harry O Maier, "A Sly Civility: Colossians and Empire," JSNT 27.3(2005)323-349.

day are in rebellion against God, driven by the "powers" and in rebellion against God and King Jesus.

Maier reviews the vocabulary, motifs, and theological themes of Colossians in relation to the cultural context of emperor worship in Asia minor. There are recognizable parallels with imperial ideas, such as the idea of rule over the whole world (Colossians 1:6), the language of a counter-triumph to the Roman imperial procession of victory known as a triumph (Colossians 2:15), and of course, the language of the kingdom of God's beloved son (Colossians 1:13). Those are just a few places where the counter-imperial language is used.

Basically, the idea is that Colossians is presenting a counter world to the Roman imperial "deity," who supposedly held all things together and provided peace and security. Maier places Colossians in special contrast to the reign of Nero, 54-68 CE, and the ideology presented during those years. Colossians is a political book, celebrating an alternate ruler, who conquered by the cross and celebrated a counter-triumph, and brings peace and reconciliation and harmony. This victory of Christ and subsequent peace is not based on bloody conquest of Roman legions bearing the standards of the empire. The language of thrones, lordships, rulers and authorities in Colossians 1:16 and 2:15, as well as the elements of the world, in Colossians 2:8 and 20, undergirded the empire, but have been defeated by the cross of Christ.

Maier suggests that Colossians presents "a sly civility," where the concord and civility, aspired to by Rome, is achieved by love in the alternate cosmic rule. Colossians has "empire renouncing logic" which "disavows the empire even as it mimics it."

Walsh and Keesmaat are along the same lines but more trenchant, bridging the modern western world of "global consumerism" and the Roman imperial world of patronage and violence. Colossians is fundamentally about reshaping the imagination of the readers, subverting both ancient and modern myths and narratives. Ethics of succession, community, liberation, and suffering replace imperial power and global consumerism. Idolatrous lies are exposed. Colossians is inviting people into a new, counter world.

In Rome, sometimes things held together, but sometimes the cracks appeared. The terrible "year of four emperors" in 69 CE, when Galba, Otho, Vitellius, and Vespasian marched against other, and legions fought each other exposed the pretense of the *Pax Romana*. At the same time, Vespasian and then Titus and his legions surrounded and destroyed Jerusalem and its temple, driving thousands into exile and slavery. There was little harmony or unity to be seen in those fateful years.

As the coronavirus epidemic, events of brutality and destruction and rioting rocked the cities of the United States in 2020, cracks in our economic, racial, and health foundations were revealed. Chaos and fear struck and stuck. Would one regime of corruption be replaced by another? Colossians presents a clear and frank picture of a world alienated from God, both individually and collectively.

The picture is of a world alienated and hostile of mind, engaged in evil deeds and lies. It is in need of reconciliation. It is driven by the evil powers and dominions, carried forth by the elements. It has failed to recognize the One for whom and through whom all things were created, whose cross brought reconciliation, and who is the head of his body the church.

Ascetic or mystical practices in quest of spiritual experiences, or the best human efforts, will not bring reconciliation and healing. The supremacy of Christ is the alternate rule that people need, were created for, and will triumph in the end by love even as it once triumphed by the cross. It is not the victory of the strong, but the victory of the One who suffered.

It is time now to briefly explore that work which entered the alienated and hostile world, the work of Christ.

CHAPTER FOUR

THE WORK OF CHRIST

A fellow student at the University of Aberdeen in Scotland once reported that he asked our professor, the renowned I. Howard Marshall, if he had any hobbies. "Christology" was the answer. Indeed, when one considers the person and work of Christ in a book like Colossians, there is enough to spend the rest of one's life pondering.

It is crucial to add here that Colossians says nothing in the terms many modern American evangelicals are used to hearing. There is nothing here about a decision, a prayer once prayed, a burst of religious enthusiasm, coming forward, or a spiritual crisis. Instead, it is about the work of Christ in the lives of the believers. It is salvation by resurrection, nothing less than Christ raising one dead in trespasses to a new life. The work of Christ is incredibly comprehensive in Colossians, one of the things which makes it such a rich book.

A crucial idea to keep front and center is that it is *God who saves in Christ*. There is no "decisionism" here, where a person is saved because he or she has prayed or raised a hand for Christ at some point. Of course, many people make decisions that are temporary or limited in duration. How long do most diets last?

The work of Christ is above all the Lord's work, not a person's decision, prayer, or even commitment. How is that work described? In this section, we will focus on the work of Christ in the transforming process, and union with Christ (the "in Christ" or "in him" or "with him" language in Colossians).

The alert reader of the other letters of Paul, however, will realize that some common themes that are prominent in other letters are either silent or very limited here. We do not find in Colossians discussions of justification by faith, the law of Moses, or Abraham, as we do in Romans and Galatians, for example. Instead, the work of Christ is highlighted in one major way. The key expression we have noted is "in Christ" or "in him" and sometimes "with Christ" or "with him" (with reference to Christ). It is union with Christ that is the key to understanding the work of Christ in Colossians (and Ephesians). New Testament theologian Udo Schnelle notes that the Greek preposition *en* is used 89 times in Colossians, the term *sōma*, or body, is used eight times, and *sun* or "with" can be found in Colossians 2:12-13, 20, 3:3 and 4.9

Schnelle approaches the subject from that of an exegete. To briefly take another example, theologian John Murray devoted a chapter of his classic reformed book *Redemption Accomplished and Applied* to union with Christ. He ranges well beyond Colossians and pushes into theological proposals not all may be comfortable with, but presents well the importance of union with Christ. He calls it the "central truth of the whole doctrine of salvation not only in its application, but also in its once-for-all accomplishment in the finished work of Christ."[10] To anticipate, he sees union with Christ as both spiritual and mystical. "Union with Christ is the central truth of the whole doctrine of salvation," says Murray. In light of the work of Christ in Colossians, that does not seem to be an overstatement.

There has been no shortage of proposals for understanding the concept of union with Christ in the NT. Sacramental, mystical, baptismal, and spatial proposals have risen, along with a myriad of other suggestions. I follow the great scholar C.F.D. Moule as seeing it rooted in the spiritual experience of the new converts at Colossae.[11]

Something happened to them and in them. They had been invaded by Christ the image of God and so were grafted within Christ. Christ's work was not now just in history, but also in and through them.

After the report of the reception and fruitfulness of the gospel in Colossians 1, and the prayer that the Colossians grow in the knowledge of God, walk worthy of the Lord, and are strengthened with divine power, we learn that it was the work of the Lord to

---

9 Udo Schnelle, *Theology of the New Testament (Grand Rapids: Baker Academic, 2007)*, p. 546.

10 John Murray, *Redemption Accomplished and Applied (Grand Rapids: Eerdmans, 2015)*, p. 171.

11 C.F.D. Moule, *The Origin of Christology (Cambridge: Cambridge University Press, 1977)*.

deliver them from the authority of darkness to Christ's kingdom, for Christ provided redemption and forgiveness of sins.

A natural starting point is the cross of Christ. After the poem which we have been speaking about in Colossians 1:15-20, it is said in verse 22 that the believers have been reconciled to present them as holy and blameless. Though once hostile and engaged in evil deeds, they have been transformed. What enables the reconciliation and transformation? It is the "the blood of the cross" in Colossians 1:20. The cross is the means of reconciliation here, while in Colossians 2:14 it was the means of removing the decrees against those who have come to believe, and in Colossians 3:3 it is a means of sanctification, as believers have died and their life is hidden with Christ in God (presumably in identity with Christ in his crucifixion). The death of Christ also creates a new situation where the elements of the world and their decrees are not binding upon believers, in Colossians 2:20. The death of Christ is multi-dimensional in its effects! We shall see that Christ's afflictions, which may involve more than the cross, are also mentioned in Colossians 1:24.

We note again here that it is the work of God to embed one in Christ. This is not done by human resolution, spiritual practice, or even devotion.

We learn that salvation is *transformation*, and the gospel is *transforming* message. It pulls a person out of one kingdom and into another, morally changing them.

It is also a partnership, or a sharing in the afflictions of Christ. There has been no shortage of ink spilled on what it means to fill up that which is lacking in Christ's afflictions in Colossians 1:24, but it is probably best to say that the suffering of believers participates in the Messiah's sufferings in a real and collective way. The work of Christ is not only toward glory, it is toward suffering. We shall return to this shortly.

Christ has invaded the lives of the Colossians. He is now "Christ among them, the hope of glory," in Colossians 1:27. They are "in Christ," subsumed in the Lord's person and identity. In a previous era, this was likened to being in water, immersed in something, but it has been realized that this takes the personhood

25

out of the matter. Believers have been placed in the sphere of the life of the person of Christ.

In Christ, rather than in esoteric speculations or disciplined practices or religious experiences involving angels, are hidden all the treasures of wisdom and knowledge (Colossians 2:3). They are to continue to walk in him, and in that wisdom in Colossians 2:6. Christ is like both the soil and the foundation of a building into which the believers are rooted.

The results of being placed "in Christ" continue in Colossians 2:9-12. All the fullness of the Godhead dwells in bodily form, the Colossian believers have been made complete, they have undergone a spiritual circumcision, and have been both buried and raised with him. Somewhat surprisingly, there is no specific mention of the cross here (as in 1:20), just Christ's burial (Colossians 2:12), in which believers have now been identified.

Christ is then the sphere and the person, the presence and the power, the identity and the source of new life in and into which the believers have been placed.

The work of Christ involves an absolute pardon, a removal of all transgressions and debt that once accrued to the Colossian believers (Colossians 1:14-15). Along with the transformation has come a cancellation!

There is also a great triumph. Christ has publicly disarmed the spiritual powers, who were created but have gone astray to evil. They are disarmed and powerless, in Colossians 2:15. This is crucial and a slightly different emphasis than the battle image of the warrior Messiah in Ephesians 6:10-20. Here in Colossians, there is actually a stripping away of the arms and strength of the defeated spiritual powers. The implication is that believers do not need to bind, or call out, or speak to evil powers. They are not hindering us from finding parking spaces or making us late to church. They have been disarmed by the work of Christ. The spiritual triumph is complete!

Christ is also the head of the church, from which all sustenance, power, and ability is given to believers. All unity comes from the head, Christ, as does all sufficiency and supply for life (Colossians 2:19). The ancient concept that the head is the source of life, growth and nourishment for the body (cf. Ephesians 4:11-16) is present here.

The work of Christ also involves turning the "shadows" into reality, specifically, the various laws regarding new moon, Sabbath, food and drink (Colossians 2:17).

Christ's exalted position is now at the right hand of God (Colossians 3:1). This was a crucial part of Christ's spiritual triumph in Ephesians 1:15-21 also. Believers are made to be "hidden" in Christ, in Colossians 3:3, having been raised up to sit with Christ. Christ will also return and be "revealed" (Colossians 3:4). Christ is our life.

Given the nature of the "image" language in the poem of Colossians 1:15, the assumption seems logical that believers are being renewed into the image of Christ in Colossians 3:10. The One who created believers, from the poem, would also be Christ, co-identified with God as creator.

Christ "is all and in all" in relation to the new unity of the body of Christ (Colossians 3:11). The peace of Christ (1:20, 3:15) is to rule amongst believers. The message about Christ is to dwell in them richly, and through Christ they are to give thanks (Colossians 3:15-17). Christ is enthroned as Lord, governing the new relationships in 3:17 and 3:20. He is to be feared in Colossians 3:22 and is the One for whom slaves are to consider that they work, in Colossians 1:23. "It is the Lord Christ whom you serve" (Colossians 1:24).

Christ is the subject of God's mystery, which must be proclaimed even more (Colossians 1:27, 4:3). The various co-workers with Paul serve "in the Lord" (4:7), which makes sense since Christ is head of the church. Archippus has received his ministry in the Lord in Colossians 4:17.

Christ was the agent of creation and the goal of creation. All things exist in, through, and for him. His death on the cross, burial, resurrection, seating, defeat of the powers and "elements," and Lordship over the universe until the time he is revealed co-exists with his indwelling the Colossian believers and community. In Christ the fullness of the deity dwells, and Christ is the head of the church who both nourishes and sustains believers. Christ is also the foundation in which they are planted. He has removed all decrees against them, and need not be sought by mystical speculations of how to be involved with angels, but is present now, in power, prayer and community. To be "in Christ" has several dimensions. It is transformational, identity giving, empowering, and community forming as well as ethic producing.

It is transforming in that it is part of the extraction of a person from the authority of darkness to the kingdom of Christ (Colossians 1:13). The person who once lived under the power of the evil forces is not in their sway anymore. They have been defeated, stripped of all power over the people of God (Colossians 2:15). Much more than a decision or moment of emotion has taken place. As a person becomes embedded in Christ, there is transformation.

A new identity is formed and given. No longer are they part of the world or the Roman empire, or their family, tribe, or nation. Now they are in Christ, and in the transnational body of Christ. Christ is their life (Colossians 3:4). Think of people who wear jerseys with their favorite team's name or logo on them, purchased on-line, showing what "tribe" they are a part of and where their money goes! Now, in and with Christ, Christ is our identity.

Life in Christ is empowering. There is a sense in which the death, burial, resurrection and seating is now part of our experience also (Colossians 2:11-12, 3:1-4). Location, authority, and status are al change, so believers live by Christ's power. Paul speaks in Colossians 1:29 of how he labors mightily, from the power that works within him. Power for endurance, prayer, witness and holiness comes from being united with Christ, embedded in him.

The new identity and power with Christ produces a different ethic of life, reordering around the kingdom of God. There is the compassion, gentleness, kindness, patience and love (Colossians 4:12), making relationships different than before. Ethics are not a subject of speculation, as with Aristotle or Plato, but part of a transformed life with a new identity and power. Everything is now done in the name of Christ, and with gratitude and thankfulness (Colossians 3:17). We will develop this in the next section.

Christ's life is now their life, since they are "in Christ" and "with Christ." The spiritual experience is real and transformative. Let us place this in context.

For those who have watched old classic movies set in ancient Rome, like *Spartacus* and *Ben Hur,* they have seen a version of the Roman empire, with lavish sets, Romans speaking with English accents, and thousands of extras. Later generations, raised on Russell Crowe as Maximus Decimus Meridius, in *Gladiator,* have seen the CGI enhanced Roman world. Those visiting ruins try and create a picture in their mind of what once was and in which the early Christians lived.

In reality, it was not romantic, glorious, or theme-park like. The Roman world was smelly, crowded, rough, and crude. Life was short and hard. No one had good teeth, skin, or eyes. People lived in *insulae,* which literally means "islands." They were crowded together without sanitation, in fire traps, and without soap or basic means of killing germs and diseases that we assume in our world. There were no aspirins, energy drinks, antidepressants, or sleep aids. One lived, suffered, and then died, possibly to be left in the streets. Many turned to magic to cope, and street hawkers taught philosophy. Few lived in the great villas we sometimes think of when we think of the Roman empire. What did they have?

The believers had the spiritually transformative experience of being implanted into Christ, the Lord of all the universe, the agent of creation, defeater of the powers, and returning king. They were raised to a new life, above and beyond what they had ever dreamed.

To say it a different way, it was not psychological help, a pep talk, or a life coach that they had discovered. The living God and his ruling Lord Jesus had invaded their lives, freed them from magic and philosophy, and "raised them with Christ." What could be better?

They also had each other now. Freed from the old patronage rituals, where you gave honor to a member of the elite who was to look out for you, you were part of a new community of love and kindness. Oh, things could go wrong, such as when Onesimus left Philemon. But, the Lord was creating a new multiethnic and transnational community where old ethnic divisions were erased in the Messiah. This was new life indeed, removal from the kingdom of darkness to the kingdom of the beloved Son. They were *together in and with Christ.*

We have just hinted at the new life that the gospel of Christ creates in people when received. How is it received, and what does it look like?

CHAPTER FIVE

NEW LIFE IN THE GOSPEL

What is the new life like in "the kingdom of his beloved son" (Colossians 1:13)? What happens for the person who has been delivered (Colossians 1:13), transferred (Colossians 1:13), redeemed (Colossians 1:14), forgiven (Colossians 1:14), reconciled (Colossians 1:22), made complete (Colossians 2:10), undergone a spiritual circumcision (Colossians 2:11), made alive (Colossians 2:13) and raised with Christ (Colossians 3:1), to name a few things from Colossians?

There is a trajectory in Colossians from the thanksgiving and prayer of ch. 1, to the greatness and sufficiency of Christ and warnings of chapter 2. In the midst of these two chapters we learn a couple of crucial things about the new life in the gospel.

First, the goal for the believer to be presented holy and blameless, without reproach, before God (Colossians 1:22). Much like Ephesians 1:4 and 5:27, this is the desired destiny for the church.

Second, Paul's goal in ministry, for which he strives with all the power God has, is to be able to present each person complete (*teleios*, just as in Matthew 5:48) in Christ. Paul is not content with mere professions of salvation, or with believers being led astray by the purported spiritual experiences, or simply holding the church at Nympha's house in Laodicea or Philemon's house in Colossae together. No! He wants, by God's grace and power, believers complete, full, mature in Christ.

There is a part for the Colossians to play also. They must continue in the faith and hope, remaining unmoved from the gospel (Colossians 1:23). In modern language, they must not "deconvert."

They must also walk in the Lord, rooted and built up (Colossians 2:7). The wonderfully mixed metaphor places them as walking trees, or mobile buildings. They have "received Christ Jesus the Lord" (Colossians 2:6). We must not mistake this with a modern altar call, or request to life one's hand or pray a prayer! The Greek word *paralambanō* is used in 1 Corinthians 15:1 and 3 for the teachings, traditions, and facts about Christ being handed down and received. It is sort of like learning a school song, school rules, school traditions, and school history all combined into one.

It is worth keeping front and central that the new life is "in Christ," as we have been emphasizing. In that sense, the scope of Colossians is unique in comparison to some other NT books. Colossians stretches from creation (Colossians 1:15-17), where all things were created in and for Christ, that Christ might have first place in everything. The letter travels through the fallen world and elements, who are defeated in the cross (2:15) and to the reconciliation made available in Christ, and which the Colossian believers have accepted (1:20, 22) and in which they must remain firm, rooted and built up in Christ. The letter travels through the afflictions believers face (1:24), their incorporation into the body of Christ (1:18, 24, 2:19), the threats from ascetic mystics touting religious experience they must avoid, all the way to the return of Christ (3:4). Colossians stretches from creation to consummation! It is in this grand and epic narrative in which the new life in Christ is situated.

The other thing to keep front and center is that the new life is lived out in and with the church. In these days of independent Christianity, attending church by watching a live-stream, and believers connected more to celebrity preachers than local assemblies, this is important to keep in focus. The Greek word "church," *ekklēsia,* means something like assembly or gathering. Since Christ is the head of the church (Colossians 1:18, 24; Ephesians 1:23), to be in Christ is to be in the church. As the reformer with the wonderful name of Oecolampadius once said, "The one who does not love the church does not love Jesus Christ."[12] The new life is not lived out by reading books on Christian ethics, but in Christ-centered believing community. Of course, this is a different view of the church than many have, assuming a community of defined faith rather than a collection of people with various religious interests.

Needless to say, as many have emphasized, the Colossian believers have not just prayed a prayer and now wait to be raptured to the clouds. They have been transferred and transformed. At the center of the great work of God in their lives is love.

---

12 Timothy George, *Reading Scripture with the Reformers (Downers Grove: InterVarsity Press, 2011),* p. 41.

One notices this right away in the letter, for in Colossians 1:4, Paul speaks of the love that they have for all the saints. Epaphras, a beloved brother, informed Paul of their Love in the Spirit (Colossians 1:8). We will later learn that Tychicus is also a beloved brother (Colossians 4:7), as is Onesimus (Colossians 4:9). Their hearts have been knit together in love (Colossians 3:2), and Paul wants them to be encouraged. They are beloved of God (Colossians 3:12).

Because of this great love that they have in Christ and are exhibiting, they also are to continue in it, putting on love like a garment, for it is the perfect bond of unity (Colossians 3:14). The previous verse connects this with forgiveness. Husbands are to love their wives (Colossians 3:19).

With this great keynote of love, two things from the ethical admonitions in Colossians may jolt readers in the present day. One relates to wives, and the other to slaves.

Colossians 3:18 says that wives should be in submission to their husbands. That hardly strikes the egalitarian note we have come to know in the 21st century in many churches!

Then, slaves are to obey their masters, not just with external conduct, but with a willing spirit (Colossians 3:22-25). What can we say about these two elements of Colossians that probably jar most modern readers?

Though no solution is perfect, nor defense completely necessary, at least two things should be kept in mind. Of course, mitigations will not be satisfying to all. The first factor to remember, though, is that the counter calls to husbands to love their wives (Colossians 3:19) and masters to be just and fair to slaves (Colossians 4:1) would be a revolutionary step forward in the first-century Roman empire. Though Colossians may not completely meet modern expectations here, it moves way beyond any other community ethic in Paul's world.

The second factor is that elsewhere in the New Testament, there are more egalitarian turns. For example, Ephesians 5:21 speaks of mutual submission between husbands and wives, not just one-way submission. Also, the letter of Philemon, where Philemon is encouraged to received back Onesimus as a "beloved brother"

33

(verse 16) may point to emancipation, perhaps even to help Paul in his old age.

We must also keep in mind that slavery in the first century was not ethnically based, as was ante-bellum American slavery in the south. Slaves sometimes had higher status and income than free people, and people even sold themselves into slavery. There is another odd twist: slaves sometimes owned other slaves! For those wanting to explore this area more, there are many fine books, but in Particular, I would recommend Jennifer A. Glancy, *Slavery in Early Christianity* (Minneapolis: Fortress, 2006) and J. Albert Harrill, *Slaves in the New Testament: Literary, Social, and Moral Dimensions* (Minneapolis: Fortress, 2006).

While the ethics of Colossians may not satisfy all, they must still be counted revolutionary in the first century.

Another crucial element of the community ethic of new life in Christ is the rejection of humanly devised religious practices. We know that religions add practices, like ships collect barnacles, as time goes on. Judaism would add the Oral Torah to the Written Torah, and of course Christianity would add various creeds, confessions and rituals throughout church history. In some sense, this process is inevitable, as new challenges are faced, and adaptations must be made.

We remember, however, that Jesus warned against holding to human tradition while neglecting or ignoring the commandments of God (Mark 7:8). Colossians follows in the wonderful train of Christian liberty in its ethics, as the letter warns against those who would create rules about tasting, handling, and observing certain religious ceremonies and days (Colossians 2:16-17, 21). Though heavily debated, the language is probably too obscure to know exactly what was being proposed, and for what reasons. Motivations for such innovations and developments may even have been positive, but innovations become traditions. Unless something is centered in the teaching of Scripture itself, adding practices and beliefs to the faith is a practice that is to be shunned. Like the Bereans in Acts 17:11, who searched the Scriptures daily to see if the things spoke of by Paul were true, believers must be diligent to examine the Scripture, and take great care to not add humanly devised traditions or practices. The new life in Christ is a life of glorious liberty and freedom in community, not one stifled with the latest innovations, suggestions, or rules.

Two other elements of the new life emerge as central in Colossians. One is prayer. It has been mentioned how Paul (and Timothy) begin with a prayer for knowledge, power, and discernment with thanksgiving (Colossians 1:9-12). Prayer is a practice that they are continually engaged in, according to Colossians 1:9. This is for a community of believers whom Paul had never met face to face!

When Paul mentions his "struggle" in 2:1, he uses the term *agōna*, that they may be encouraged, with their hearts knit together. He is probably talking about prayer here. The same term is used in the participle form in Colossians 4:12, where it describes how Epaphras, the founder of the church, is always *agonizing* (Greek *agōnizomenos*) for them in his prayers, that they may be complete and fully assured in the will of God. Those two elements echo the prayer of chapter 1, especially verse 9, and the goal of Paul's ministry in 1:28, to present every person complete in Christ.

There is the encouragement for the Colossian believers to devote themselves to prayer in Colossians 4:2-4. They are to be watchful and alert in prayer, with thanksgiving, especially praying for Paul to be clear in his preaching and for God to open new doors for the word. The interconnection of prayer for believers and those away at a distance wonderfully exhibits the unity of the body of Christ. One imagines them gathering several evenings out of the week for times of prayer, and beginning their days with a short time of prayer, learning both from the examples of Jesus they were taught, the models Epaphras gave them, the Psalms, and now Paul's prayers in this letter. The new life in Christ can never be a prayerless life. Like the Israelite/Jewish tradition they have inherited, prayer is central, only now it is of even greater richness, because they are seated with Christ at God's right hand (Colossians 3:1)!

Suffering is another central and yet inevitable part of the new life. Though scholars have debated the relation of emperor worship to active persecution or social pressure, this topic is not front and center in all the NT books, nor in all the letters of Paul. However, it is assumed that "the sufferings of the present time are not worthy to be compared with the glories that are to be revealed to us" (Romans 8:18). Paul himself would narrate some of his sufferings in passages like 2 Corinthians 11:22-29 as a mark of his apostolic call. Suffering comes into Colossians in at least three ways, as the present evil age collides with the invasion of the kingdom of God.

First of all, Paul himself is in prison, along with Aristarchus, according to Colossians 4:3, 10 and 18. We have mentioned earlier the uncertainty as to the location of the imprisonment, with Ephesus and Rome being the main candidates, and Caesarea a remote third, but it is unmistakable that Colossians ranks as one of the "prison letters." Especially if from Ephesus, it is astounding to think of the majestic poem of 1:15-20 emerging from a dark, wet, dank cave-like cell.

A second way that suffering comes into the letter is the mention that Paul rejoices in his suffering in Colossians 1:24. This note of joy is obviously meant to be an example for the Colossians, as Colossians 3:16 makes clear. Much like Philippians, Paul practices and wants to model "joy in the Lord" (Philippians 4:4).

A third way that suffering comes into Colossians connects with what we mentioned earlier, the mysterious statement in Colossians 1:24, where Paul says he is filling up what is lacking in the Messiah's afflictions. Scads of ink has been spilled over what exactly this might mean, and I have no great light to shed on it. However, the idea is probably that in identification with the Messiah, the Messiah's people like Paul continue the process of suffering, not in an atoning way, but in a true identification and continuation with the suffering of God's servant (Isaiah 42, 53). That suffering will continue until the kingdom of God has its final triumph.

This is all possible for now because of the surprising location of their lives. They have died, and their life is hidden with Christ in God (Colossians 2:20, 3:3). Then, they are raised with Christ and seated at the right hand of God (Colossians 3:1). The result is that they seek the things that are "above." They don't really care about gladiator games, chariot races, banquets at the temples, or the various entertainments and politics of the Roman world. They are in Christ's kingdom!

They also live with severity, "putting to death" or "mortifying" as older translations put it, various poisonous and sinful elements of their old lives, such as fornication, greed, anger, impurity, lies, and malice (Colossians 3:5-10). They know such things are part of the old life and old creation, and they are new, living the life of the kingdom of Christ that will one day fill the whole world!

THE COLOSSIAN GOSPEL

This small, young church, with its odd assortment of people, with their bad skin and bad teeth, in the midst of short and difficult lives, in a town that life was passing by in the Roman empire, have found themselves part of a very large story. Indeed, it is the greatest and most true story ever told. It is the story of the redemption and reconciliation of the universe under the kingship of Jesus. He is the One for whom everything was originally intended.

It is the good news that we, like Epaphras, must spread in its fullness. It is not about getting someone to raise their hand in a dark building after listening to a rock band; it is about being invaded by Christ, jolted into Christ's kingdom, and living in love, faith, and prayer in this new, transnational community. The focus? It is not spiritual experiences and rules, but the supremacy, greatness, and majesty of Jesus Christ.[13]

---

13 For further study, I recommend Scot McKnight, *Colossians* (NICNT; Grand Rapids: Eerdmans, 2018); Douglas Moo, *The Letters to the Colossians and Philemon* (Pillar NT Commentaries; Grand Rapids: Eerdmans, 2008); N.T. Wright, *Colossians and Philemon* (Tyndale NT Commentaries; Downers Grove: IVP, 2008); C.F.D. Moule, *The Epistles to the Colossians and Philemon* (Cambridge Greek Testament Commentary; Cambridge: Cambridge University Press, 1957).

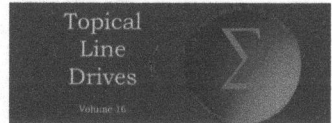

* 9 7 8 1 6 3 1 9 9 7 3 4 1 *